PIANO / VOCAL / GUITAR

THE BEST OF PASSION

ISBN 978-1-4768-1267-0

7777 W. BLUEMOUND RD. P.O. BOX 13819 MILWAUKEE, WI 53213

Visit Hal Leonard Online at
www.halleonard.com

CONTENTS

ALWAYS

Words and Music by JASON INGRAM
and KRISTIAN STANFILL

Recorded a half step lower.

AMAZING GRACE
(My Chains Are Gone)

Words by JOHN NEWTON
Traditional American Melody
Additional Words and Music by CHRIS TOMLIN
and LOUIE GIGLIO

AWAKENING

Words and Music by REUBEN MORGAN
and CHRIS TOMLIN

Like the ris - ing ___ sun ___

___ that shines, ___ from the dark - ness ___ comes ___ a light. ___

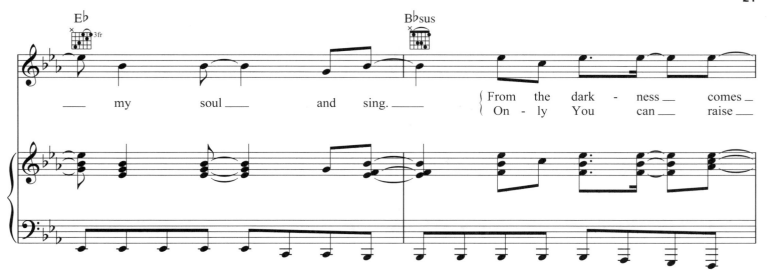

my soul ___ and sing. ___ { From the dark - ness ___ comes ___
{ On - ly You can ___ raise ___

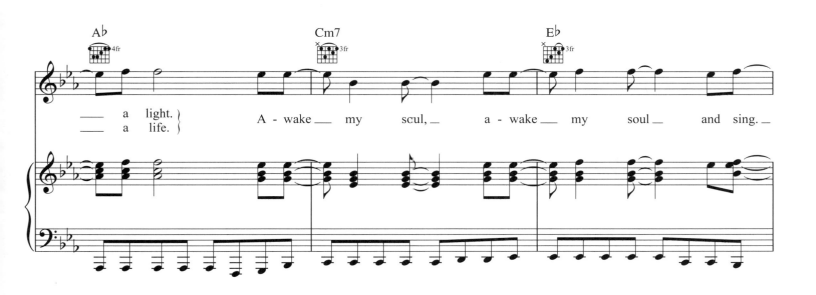

___ a light. }
___ a life. } A - wake ___ my soul, ___ a - wake ___ my soul ___ and sing. ___

___ Like the ris - ing ___ sun ___ ___

AWESOME IS THE LORD MOST HIGH

Words and Music by CHRIS TOMLIN,
JESSE REEVES, CARY PIERCE
and JON ABEL

Moderately fast

Great are You, ___ Lord, ___
Where You send ___ us, ___

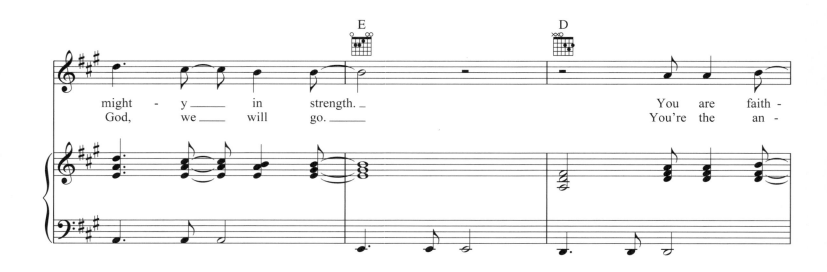

might - y ___ in strength. ___ You are faith -
God, we ___ will go. ___ You're the an -

BETTER IS ONE DAY

Words and Music by
MATT REDMAN

BE GLORIFIED

Words and Music by LOUIE GIGLIO,
CHRIS TOMLIN and JESSE REEVES

BLESSED BE YOUR NAME

Words and Music by MATT REDMAN
and BETH REDMAN

* *Recorded a half step lower.*

GIVE US CLEAN HANDS

Words and Music by
CHARLIE HALL

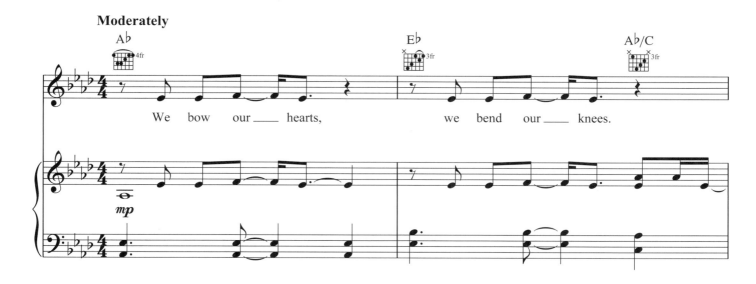

We bow our ___ hearts, we bend our ___ knees.

O Spir- it, come make us hum - ble. We turn our ___ eyes

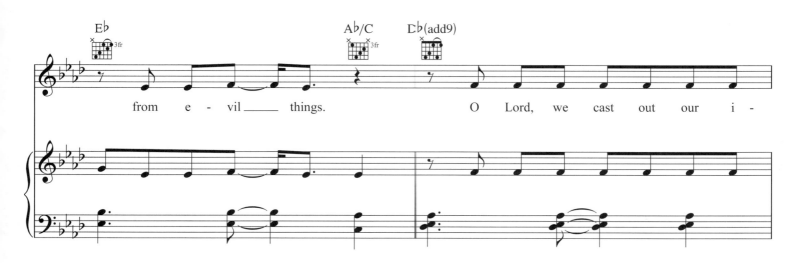

from e - vil ___ things. O Lord, we cast out our i -

DID YOU FEEL THE MOUNTAINS TREMBLE?

Words and Music by
MARTIN SMITH

ENOUGH

Words and Music by CHRIS TOMLIN
and LOUIE GIGLIO

Steadily

All of You is more than e - nough

for all of me, for ev-'ry thirst and ev-'ry need.

You sat-is-fy me with Your love, and all I have in You

EVERYTHING GLORIOUS

Words and Music by
DAVID CROWDER

Moderately

The day __ is bright - er here __ with You. __
My eyes __ are small, __ but they __ have seen __

The night __ is light - er than __ its hue __
the beau - ty of __ e - nor - mous things, __

would lead __ me to be - lieve,
which leads __ me to be - lieve

which leads __ me to
there's light __ e - nough

Recorded a half step lower.

62

You are glo-ri-ous, _____ You are glo-ri-ous, _____

You are glo-ri-ous, _____ You are glo-ri-ous. _____

FAMOUS ONE

Words and Music by CHRIS TOMLIN
and JESSE REEVES

GRACE FLOWS DOWN

Words and Music by LOUIE GIGLIO,
DAVID BELL and ROD PADGETT

GOD OF THIS CITY

Words and Music by AARON BOYD,
PETER COMFORT, RICHARD BLEAKLEY,
PETER KERNAGHAN, ANDREW McCANN
and IAN JORDAN

* Recorded a half step lower.

HEALING IS IN YOUR HANDS

Words and Music by DANIEL CARSON,
CHRIS TOMLIN, CHRISTY NOCKELS,
MATT REDMAN and NATHAN NOCKELS

HERE FOR YOU

Words and Music by TIMOTHY WANSTALL,
MATT REDMAN, MATT MAHER and JESSE REEVES

* Recorded a half step lower.

HOW HE LOVES

Words and Music by
JOHN MARK McMILLAN

HERE IS OUR KING

Words and Music by
DAVID CROWDER

HOLY IS THE LORD

Words and Music by CHRIS TOMLIN
and LOUIE GIGLIO

HOW GREAT IS OUR GOD

Words and Music by CHRIS TOMLIN,
JESSE REEVES and ED CASH

HOW MARVELOUS

Words and Music by
CHRIS TOMLIN

JESUS PAID IT ALL

Words and Music by
ALEX NIFONG

Recorded a half step lower.

JESUS, SON OF GOD

Words and Music by CHRIS TOMLIN,
MATT MAHER and JASON INGRAM

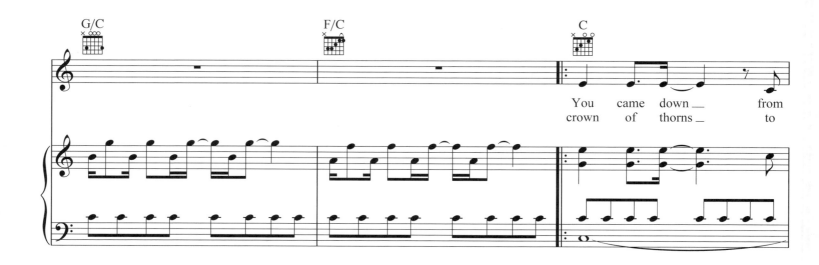

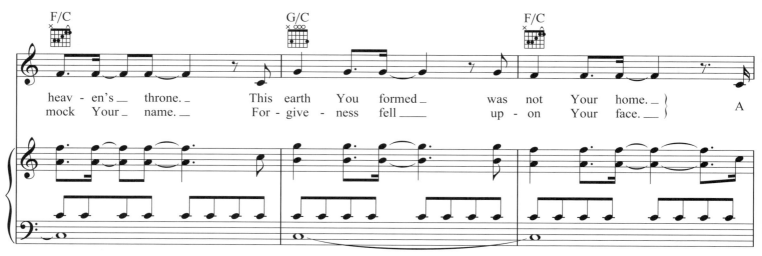

Recorded a half step lower.

LET EVERYTHING THAT HAS BREATH

Words and Music by
MATT REDMAN

THE LORD OUR GOD

Words and Music by JASON INGRAM
and KRISTIAN STANFILL

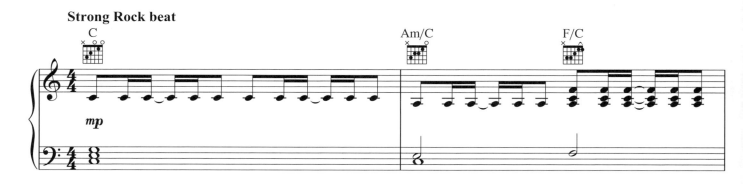

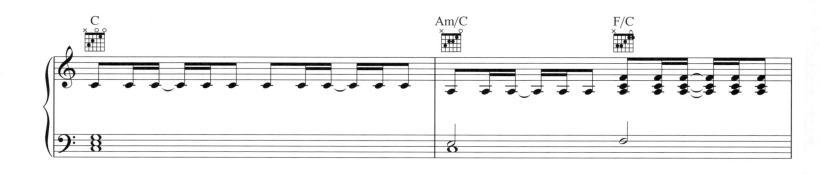

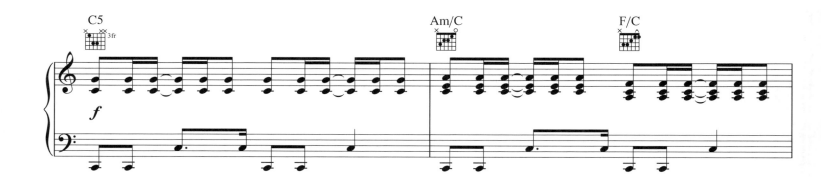

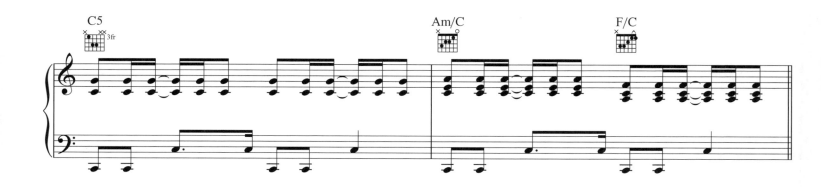

A MIGHTY FORTRESS

Words and Music by CHRISTY NOCKELS
and NATHAN NOCKELS

Moderate Ballad

Our God is a con-sum-ing ___ fire, a burn-ing ho-ly ___
God is jeal-ous for His ___ own, none could com-pre-

___ flame with glo-ry and free - dom. Our God is the on-ly right-eous
- hend His love and His mer - cy. Our God is ex-alt-ed on His ___

___ judge, rul-ing o-ver us ___ with kind-ness and wis - dom. }
___ throne, high a-bove the heav - ens, for-ev-er He's wor - thy. } We will keep our

Recorded a half step lower.

MARVELOUS LIGHT

Words and Music by
CHARLIE HALL

* Recorded a half step lower.

MY HEART IS YOURS

Words and Music by JASON INGRAM,
KRISTIAN STANFILL, DANIEL CARSON
and BRETT YOUNKER

O PRAISE HIM
(All This for a King)

Words and Music by
DAVID CROWDER

OUR GOD

Words and Music by JONAS MYRIN,
CHRIS TOMLIN, MATT REDMAN
and JESSE REEVES

And if our God is for us, then who could ev - er stop us? And if our God is with us,

RISE AND SING

Words and Music by
STEVE FEE

If you're a - live and you've been re - deemed, ____ rise ____ and sing, ____ rise ____
If you were bound but now ____ you're free, ____ rise ____ and sing, ____ rise ____
If in your heart rings a mel - o - dy, ____ rise ____ and sing, ____ rise ____

*Recorded a half step lower.

Let the re-deemed of the Lord sing: Hal - le - lu - jah. (Hal - le - lu -

- jah.) Let the re-deemed of the Lord sing: Our God

ONE THING REMAINS
(Your Love Never Fails)

Words and Music by JEREMY RIDDLE,
BRIAN JOHNSON and CHRISTA BLACK

High - er than the moun - tains that I _____ face,

strong - er than the pow - er of the _____ grave,   con - stant in the tri - al and the _____

_____ change,   this one thing   re - mains, _____   this one

* *Recorded a half step lower.*

never fails, it nev-er gives up, it nev-er runs out on me. Your love

never fails, it nev-er gives up, it nev-er runs out on me. Your love

never fails, it nev-er gives up, it nev-er runs out on me, Your

love. In death, in life, I'm

SING SING SING

Words and Music by CHRIS TOMLIN,
JESSE REEVES, DANIEL CARSON,
TRAVIS NUNN and MATT GILDER

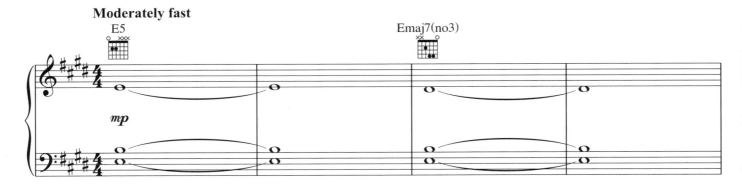

Sing, sing, sing, ____ and make mu-

10,000 REASONS
(Bless the Lord)

Words and Music by JONAS MYRIN
and MATT REDMAN

Moderate Ballad

Bless the Lord, O my soul, O _____ my soul.

Wor-ship His ho-ly name. ___ Sing like nev-er be-fore,

O my soul. I'll wor-ship Your ho-ly name. ___

WHITE FLAG

Words and Music by CHRIS TOMLIN,
MATT REDMAN, MATT MAHER
and JASON INGRAM

Moderate Rock beat

The bat-tle rag - es __ on __ as storm and tem - pest __ roar. __

We can - not win this __ fight __

WAITING HERE FOR YOU

Words and Music by CHRIS TOMLIN,
JESSE REEVES and MARTIN SMITH

Passionately

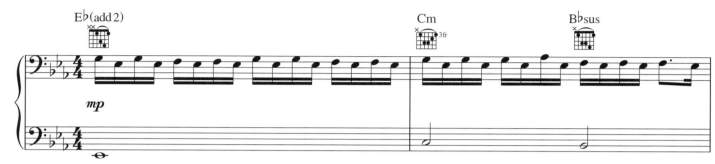

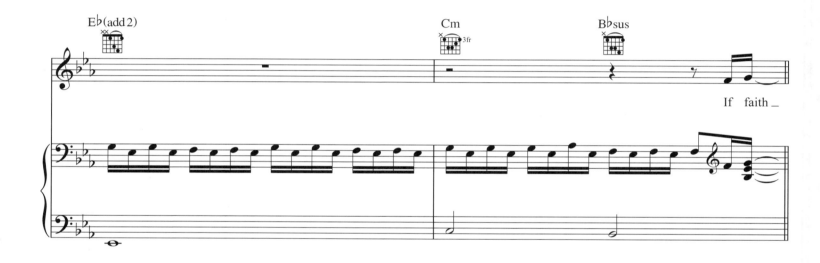

If faith __

__ can move __ the moun - tains, let __ the moun - tains move. __ We come
__ of all __ cre - a - tion, and still __ You know __ my heart. __ The Au -
- 'ry - thing __ You've prom - ised; Your faith - ful - ness __ is true. __ We're des -

WHOM SHALL I FEAR
(God of Angel Armies)

Words and Music by CHRIS TOMLIN,
ED CASH and SCOTT CASH

WE FALL DOWN

Words and Music by
CHRIS TOMLIN

YOU ALONE

Words and Music by JACK PARKER
and DAVID CROWDER

(1., 3.) You _____ are the on - ly _____ One I _____ need. _____ I bow
(2., 4.) You _____ have giv - en me _____ more than _____ I _____ could

all of me _____ at Your _____ feet. _____ I
ev - er have _____ want - ed, ___ and I _____ want to

wor - ship _____ You a - lone.
give You my _____ heart and my _____ soul.

YOU ALONE CAN RESCUE

Words and Music by JONAS MYRIN
and MATT REDMAN

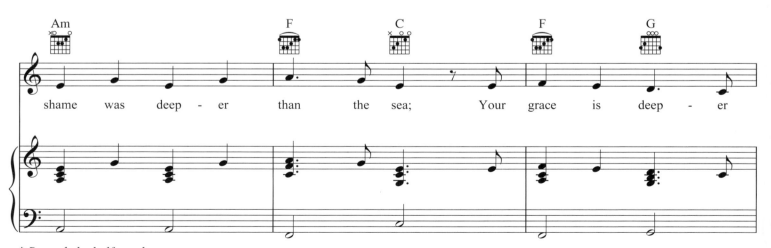

Recorded a half step lower.

YOU ARE MY KING
(Amazing Love)

Words and Music by
BILLY JAMES FOOTE

YOU NEVER LET GO

Words and Music by MATT REDMAN
and BETH REDMAN

Recorded a half step lower.

Yes, I can see a light that is com-ing for the heart that holds on. ____ And there will be an end to these trou-bles, but un-til that day comes, __ still I will praise You, still I will praise You. _____